The Best Mum in the World

THIS IS A PRION BOOK

First published in Great Britain in 2016 by Prion
An imprint of the Carlton Publishing Group
20 Mortimer Street
London W1T 3JW

A CIP catalogue for this book is available from the British Library.

ISBN 978-1-85375-951-2

Printed in Dubai

10 9 8 7 6 5 4 3

The Best Mum in the World

Humorous and Inspirational Quotes
Celebrating Marvellous Mothers

PRION

Contents

Introduction

Motherhood – it's the toughest job in the world. Who else has to utilise the skills of the nurse, drill sergeant, chef, referee, banker, telephonist and politician – all before nine in the morning? But as unthanked, unpaid careers go, it's pretty good, for the salary is pure gold – a child's eternal love.

This collection of quotes on mums captures the words of wits, sages and celebrities across the ages. From James Joyce to Angelina Jolie, expressions of love and gratitude dovetail with pin-point observations and hilarious, caustic one-liners. Whether you're searching for the perfect sentiment for your own mother, reading in excited expectation of having your own child or just enjoy browsing the brilliant words of others, you'll find so much to enjoy in this fabulous selection.

A Mother's Love

"A suburban mother's role is to deliver children obstetrically once, and by car forever after."

Peter de Vries

"You make sacrifices to become a mother. But you really find yourself and your soul when you are one."

Mariska Hargitay

"It's not easy being a mother. If it were easy, fathers would do it."

Dorothy, *The Golden Girls*

"A mother is a person who's seeing there are only four pieces of pie for five people, promptly announces she never did care for pie."

Tenneva Jordan

"I realized when you look at your mother, you are looking at the purest love you will ever know."

Mitch Albom

"The only love that I really believe in is a mother's love for her children."

Karl Lagerfeld

"Motherhood is not for the fainthearted. Frogs, skinned knees and the insults of teenage girls are not meant for the wimpy."

Danielle Steel

"A mother is someone who
dreams great dreams for you, but
then she lets you chase the dreams
you have for yourself and loves you
just the same."

Anon

"I owe her much. I feel deeply
that I am the son of woman.
Every instant, in my ideas and
words (not to mention my features
and gestures), I find again my
mother in myself."

Samuel Smiles

"A mother is the one who is still there when everyone else has deserted you."

Anon

"I will look after you and I will look after anybody you say needs to be looked after, any way you say. I am here. I brought my whole self to you. I am your mother."

Maya Angelou

"A mother's love for her child is like nothing else in the world. It knows no law, no pity, it dates all things and crushes down remorselessly all that stands in its path."

Agatha Christie

"There is only one pretty child in the world, and every mother has it."

Chinese proverb

"It's the job that I take most seriously in my life and I think it's the hardest job."

Debra Messing

"Most of us would do more for our babies than we have ever been willing to do for anyone, even ourselves."

Polly Berrien Berends

"There is an instinct in a woman to love most her own child – and an instinct to make any child who needs her love, her own."

Robert Brault

"Mother's love is bliss, is peace, it need not be acquired, it need not be deserved. If it is there, it is like a blessing; if it is not there it is as if all the beauty had gone out of life."

Erich Fromm

"A mother is the truest friend
we have, when trials heavy and
sudden fall upon us; when adversity
takes the place of prosperity; when
friends desert us; when trouble
thickens around us, still will she
cling to us, and endeavor by her
kind precepts and counsels to
dissipate the clouds of darkness,
and cause peace to return
to our hearts."

Washington Irving

"I want my children to have all the things I couldn't afford. Then I want to move in with them."

Phyllis Diller

"Grown don't mean nothing to a mother. A child is a child. They get bigger, older, but grown? What's that suppose to mean? In my heart it don't mean a thing."

Toni Morrison

"I love my mother as the trees love water and sunshine – she helps me grow, prosper and reach great heights."

Adabella Radici

"A woman knows all about her children. She knows about dental appointments and football games and romances and best friends and favourite foods and secret fears and hopes and dreams. A man is vaguely aware of some short people living in the house."

Dave Berry

"'I always wondered why God was supposed to be a father,' she whispers. 'Fathers always want you to measure up to something. Mothers are the ones who love you unconditionally, don't you think?'"

Jodi Picoult

"Whatever else is unsure in this stinking dunghill of a world a mother's love is not."

James Joyce

"You rock a sobbing child without wondering if today's world is passing you by, because you know you hold tomorrow tightly in your arms."

Neal A. Maxwell

"No one can take the place of a perfect mother who gives you the world as you know it and makes you believe that it is yours to take."

Tristan Wood

"The clocks were striking midnight and the rooms were very still as a figure glided quietly from bed to bed, smoothing a coverlid here, settling a pillow there, and pausing to look long and tenderly at each unconscious face, to kiss each with lips that mutely blessed, and to pray the fervent prayers which only mothers utter."

Louisa May Alcott, Little Women

"She is the creature of life, the giver of life, and the giver of abundant love, care and protection. Such are the great qualities of a mother. The bond between a mother and her child is the only real and purest bond in the world, the only true love we can ever find in our lifetime."

Ama H. Vanniarachchy

"Mother's hug – the only drug that works every time, costs nothing and has no side effects."

Hassaan Ali

"No one else will ever know the strength of my love for you. After all, you're the only one who knows what my heart sounds like from the inside."

Anon

"The common language shared by everyone in this world is the cry which only our mothers understood."

Gopichand Lagadapati

A Mother Is...

"Being a mom made me realize that motherhood is an impossibly difficult task. It's also made me make a motto around our house: I'm not perfect and I don't expect you to be. We do the best we can."

Rena Sofer

"Being a mom made me stronger. I'm a warrior!"

Garcelle Beauvais

"Oh what a power is motherhood,
possessing a potent spell!"

Euripedes

"Being a full-time mother is one of
the highest salaried jobs in my field,
since the payment is pure love."

Mildred B. Vermont

"The one thing you've got to be
prepared to do as a parent is not to
be liked from time to time."

Emma Thompson

"What makes mothers all that they are? Might as well ask, 'What makes a star?' Ask your heart to tell you her worth. Your heart will say, 'Heaven on earth.'"

Peter Pan, Disney

"Being a mother is an attitude, not a biological relation."

Robert A. Heinlein

"A mother is a child's first looking glass into the world."

Richelle E. Goodrich

"A mother is always the beginning.
She is how things begin."

Amy Tan

"If I were asked to define
motherhood, I would have defined
it as love in its purest form.
Unconditional love."

Revathi Sankaran

"Being a mom has made me
so tired. And so happy."

Tina Fey

31

"A mother is neither cocky nor proud, because she knows that the school principle may call at any minute to report that her child has just driven a motorcycle through the gymnasium."

Mary Kay Blakely

"A mother is not a person to lean on, but a person to make leaning unnecessary."

Dorothy Canfield Fisher

"Kids don't stay with you if you do it right. It's the one job where, the better you are, the more surely you won't be needed in the long run."

Barbara Kingsolver

"Being a mom made me realize that life is an adventure. No two days are ever the same, which is so exciting."

Jada Pinkett Smith

"Biology is the least of what makes someone a mother."

Oprah Winfrey

"All mothers are slightly insane."

J.D. Salinger

"Motherhood.
Powered by love.
Fuelled by coffee.
Sustained by wine."

Anon

"Motherhood has a very humanizing effect. Everything gets reduced to essentials."

Meryl Streep

"Motherhood is a choice you make every day, to put someone else's happiness and well-being ahead of your own, to teach the hard lessons, to do the right thing even when you're not sure what the right thing is... and to forgive yourself, over and over again, for doing everything wrong."

Donna Ball

"Motherhood is near to divinity. It is the highest holiest service to be assumed by mankind."

Howard W. Hunter

"Children are like sponges; they absorb all your strength and leave you limp... But give them a squeeze and you get it all back."

Barbara Johnson

"Motherhood is neither a duty nor a privilege, but simply the way that humanity can satisfy the desire for physical immortality and triumph over the fear of death."

Rebecca West

"Very early on in writing the series, I remember a female journalist saying to me that Mrs Weasley, 'Well, you know, she's just a mother.' And I was absolutely incensed by that comment."

J.K. Rowling

Mothers and Motherhood

"I am sure that if the mothers of various nations could meet, there would be no more wars."

E.M. Forster

"All women become like their mothers. That is their tragedy. No man does. That's his."

Oscar Wilde

"I'd like to be the ideal mother, but I'm too busy raising my kids."

Anon

"Guilt is to motherhood as grapes are to wine."

Fay Weldon

"As long as a woman can look ten years younger than her own daughter, she is perfectly satisfied."

Oscar Wilde

"A good mother is irreplaceable."

Adriana Trigiani

"I can hear my conscience rapping to me. It's like, 'Hey, you've only got one real friend'. From the cradle, to the grave, and back again. With unconditional love, that's my mother I'm speakin' of."

The Insane Clown Posse, The Mom Song

"Youth fades; love droops; the leaves of friendship fall; a mother's secret hope outlives them all."

Oliver Wendell Holmes, Sr.

"A daughter without her mother
is a woman broken. It is a loss that
turns to arthritis and settles deep
into her bones."

Kristin Hannah

"Clarity and focus doesn't always
come from God or inspirational
quotes. Usually, it takes your mother
to slap the reality back into you."

Shannon L. Alder

"If you remember yourself, you will remember me. I am always a part of you. I am your mother."

Emma Michaels

"Don't listen to anyone's advice. Listen to your baby… There are so many books, doctors, and well-meaning friends and family. We like to say, 'You don't need a book. Your baby is a book. Just pick it up and read it.'"

Mayim Bialik

"Everybody wants to save the earth; nobody wants to help mom do the dishes."

P.J. O'Rourke

"If I were hanged on the highest hill, mother o' mine, O mother o' mine! I know whose love would follow me still, mother o' mine, O mother o' mine!"

Rudyard Kipling

"A good mother loves fiercely, but ultimately brings up her children to thrive without her. They must be the most important thing in her life, but if she is the most important thing in theirs, she has failed."

Erin Kelly

"A little girl, asked where her home was, replied, 'Where mother is.'"

Keith L. Brooks

"Don't forget Mother's Day. Or, as they call it in Beverley Hills, Dad's Third Wife Day."

Jay Leno

"A man loves his sweetheart the most, his wife the best, but his mother the longest."

Irish proverb

"Because I am a mother, I am incapable of being shocked as I never was when I was not one."

Margaret Atwood

"I don't know what it is about food your mother makes for you, especially when it's something that anyone can make – pancakes, meat loaf, tuna salad – but it carries a certain taste of memory."

Mitch Albom

"Art is the child of nature in whom we trace the features of the mother's face."

Henry Wadsworth Longfellow

"You couldn't fool your mother on the foolingest day of your life if you had an electrified fooling machine."

Homer Simpson

"As mothers and daughters, we are connected with one another. My mother is the bones of my spine, keeping me straight and true. She is my blood, making sure it runs rich and strong. She is the beating of my heart. I cannot now imagine a life without her."

Kristin Hannah

"I believe in the strength and intelligence and sensitivity of women. My mother, my sisters [they] are strong. My mum is a strong woman and I love her for it."

Tom Hiddleston

"I know enough to know that no woman should ever marry a man who hated his mother."

Martha Gellhorn

"At the end of the day, can you look back and say to yourself, 'Today, my mother would be proud of me because I gave it all I had?' If you can, you will have had a very good day. And if you can do this every day, you will have a very good life."

Patrick Henry Hughes

"If evolution really works, how come mothers only have two hands?"

Milton Berle

"Before becoming a mother I had a hundred theories on how to bring up children. Now I have seven children and only one theory: love them, especially when they least deserve to be loved."

Kate Samperi

"Even as a small child, I understood that women had secrets, and that some of these were only to be told to daughters. In this way we were bound together for eternity."

Alice Hoffman

"I ask you, what good is a big picture window and the lavish appointments and a priceless decor in a home if there is no mother there?"

Spencer W. Kimball

"No matter how knowledgeable you are, respect your parents for their experience and your children for their curiosity."

Amit Kalantri

"Only mothers can think of the future − because they give birth to it in their children."

Maxim Gorky

"People always talk about a mother's uncanny ability to read her children, but that was nothing compared to how children could read their mothers."

Anne Tyler

"The best love in the world is the love of a man. The love of a man who came from your womb, the love of your son! I don't have a daughter, but maybe the love of a daughter is the best, too. I am first and foremost me, but right after that I am a mother. The best thing that I can ever be is me. But the best gift that I will ever have is being a mother."

C. JoyBell C.

"The best medicine in the world is a mother's kiss."

Anon

"Now, as always, the most
automated appliance in a household
is the mother."

Beverly Jones

"The best place to cry is on a
mother's arms."

Jodi Picoult

"Nothing will ever make you as
happy or sad, as proud or tired,
as motherhood."

Elia Parsons

"The commonest fallacy among women is that simply having children makes them a mother – which is as absurd as believing that having a piano makes one a musician."

Sidney J. Harris

"The greatest thing a father can do for his children is to respect the woman that gave birth to his children. It is because of her that you have the greatest treasures in your life."

Shannon L. Alder

"The hand that rocks the cradle is the hand that rules the world."

W. R. Wallace

"There is no velvet so soft as a mother's lap, no rose as lovely as her smile, no path so flowery as that imprinted with her footsteps."

Archibald Thompson

"Our mothers always remain the strangest, craziest people we've ever met."

Marguerite Duras

"The one thing children wear out faster than shoes is parents."

John L. Plomp

"The story of a mother's life:
trapped between a scream
and a hug."

Cathy Guisewite

"There is no one who takes care of
us as lovingly as our mother does.
She is our living God."

Mohtasham Usmani

"There is nothing as sincere
as a mother's kiss."

Saleem Sharma

"There's no way to be a perfect
mother and a million ways to be
a good one."

Jill Churchill

"There's nothing like your mother's
sympathetic voice to make you want
to burst into tears."

Sophie Kinsella

"They are not kidding when they say that mothers are strong women. We need to be strong in more ways than our children will ever know."

M. B. Antevasin

"You may have tangible wealth untold; caskets of jewels and coffers of gold. Richer than I you can never be, I had a mother who read to me."

Strickland Gillilan

"Of all the rights of women the greatest is to be a mother."

Lyn Yutan

"The world is full of women blindsided by the unceasing demands of motherhood, still flabbergasted by how a job can be terrific and tortuous."

Anna Quindlen

"Every beetle is a gazelle in the eyes of its mother."

Arab proverb

"A mother is a woman with a 25-hour day who can still find time to play with her family."

Iris Peck

"Childhood smells of perfume and brownies."

David Leavitt

"A mother is like a pavement in the middle of the fast lane."

Anon

"Think of your mother and smile for all of the good, precious moments."

Ana Monnar

Celebrities
and Their
Mums

"My mom and I have always been really close. She's always been the friend that was always there. There were times when, in middle school and junior high, I didn't have a lot of friends. But my mom was always my friend. Always."

Taylor Swift

"Can't you see you're like a book of poetry? Maya Angelou, Nicky Giovanni. Turn one page and there's my mommy."

Kanye West, Hey Mama

"I get my sense of humor from my mom. There are so many quiet times you spend as a mother that aren't glorified, but are a foundation for your kids. No matter what, there was always a thick safety net under this trapeze."

Tina Fey

"I just can't forget how you gave me love, oh no. If there's a heaven up above know she's teaching angels how to love."

R Kelly, Sadie

"My mom means a lot to me. My mom gave up everything. She moved with me and believed in me. She is awesome."

Justin Bieber

"If I have done anything in life worth attention, I feel sure that I inherited the disposition from my mother."

Booker T. Washington

"My mother is everything to me. She's my anchor, she's the person I go to when I need to talk to someone. She is an amazing woman."

Demi Lovato

"I'm still amazed at how my mother emerged from her lonely early life as such an affectionate and level-headed woman."

Hillary Clinton

"My mother never saw the irony in calling me a son-of-a-bitch."

Jack Nicholson

"So mother, I thank you
for all that you've done and still do.
You got me, I got you.
Together we always pull through."

Christine Aguilera, Oh Mother

"Even when I go out with my mom
I don't look at other moms."

Garry Shandling

"There is a video I found from back when I was three. You set up a paint set in the kitchen and you're talking to me. It's the age of princesses and pirate ships and the seven dwarfs. And Daddy's smart and you're the prettiest lady in the whole wide world."

Taylor Swift, The Best Day

"I felt my mother about the place. I don't think she haunts me, but I wouldn't put it past her."

Julie Walters

"She wanted me to work in the post office. She begged me to take a civil service test. I don't think I would have made a good postman... I could have put up with the rain and the snow. The hail – forget it."

Larry David

"[My mom] had this amazing attitude in the face of everything, including when she got cancer."

Bill Clinton

"[My mom] is one of those people that you feel honored to meet. And no matter who you are, you fall in love with her because she is spiritual, she's inspiring, she's strong, she's funny, she's creative, she's talented... She's everything that I want to be."

Beyoncé

"When I hear the Sunday
bells ringing in the morning
I remember crying when she used to
sing. Oh, Mama liked the roses but
most of all she cared about the
way we learned to live and if we
said our prayers."

Elvis Presley, Mama Liked the Roses

"She raised us with humor and she
raised us to understand that not
everything was going to be great –
but how to laugh through it."

Liza Minnelli

"[What's beautiful about my mother is] her compassion, how much she gives, whether it be to her kids and grandkids or out in the world. She's got a sparkle."

Kate Hudson on mom Goldie Hawn

"My mother never gave up on me. I messed up in school so much they were sending me home, but my mother sent me right back."

Denzel Washington

"I finally understand. For a woman it ain't easy trying to raise a man. You always was committed. A poor single mother on welfare, tell me how ya did it. There's no way I can pay you back, but the plan is to show you that I understand. You are appreciated."

Tupac Shakur, Dear Mama

"Over the years, I learned so much from mom. She taught me about the importance of home and history and family and tradition. She also taught me that ageing need not mean narrowing the scope of your activities and interests or a diminution of the great pleasures to be had in the everyday."

Martha Stewart

"She drove me to ballet class…
and she took me to every audition.
She'd be proud of me if I was
still sitting in that seat or if I was
watching from home. She believes
in me and that's why this [award] is
for her. She's a wonderful mother."

Elisabeth Moss

"I unapologetically and
unabashedly am deeply biased
toward my mother."

Chelsea Clinton

"You showed me when I was young just how to grow. You showed me everything that I should know. You showed me just how to walk without your hands, cuz mom you always were the perfect fan."

The Backstreet Boys, The Perfect Fan

"No man is poor who has a godly mother."

Abraham Lincoln

"I remember being seven and asking my mom if I was as pretty as Monique (my best friend in grade school). And with all the love in the world, my mom looked at me and said, 'Oh, honey, you're so funny.' So, she doesn't lie to me... she answers the question by not answering and instead tells me what she thinks is my greatest strength."

Jennifer Aniston

"In 1971, Bossier City, Louisiana, there was a teenage girl who was pregnant with her second child. She was a high school dropout and a single mom, but somehow she managed to make a better life for herself and her children. She encouraged her kids to be creative, to work hard, and to do something special. That girl is my mother and she's here tonight. And I just want to say, I love you, Mom. Thank you for teaching me to dream."

Jared Leto

"Mama, you taught me to do the right things, so now you have to let your baby fly. You've given me everything that I will need to make it through this crazy thing called life."

Carrie Underwood

"My mother has always been unhappy with what I do. She would rather I do something nicer, like be a bricklayer."

Mick Jagger

"My parents divorced when I was eight, and whenever I felt down, my mom would remind me that a sense of humor gets you through just about anything."

Julia Louis-Dreyfus

"My mother is a walking miracle."

Leonardo DiCaprio

"My parents elected me president
of the family when I was four.
We actually had an election every
year and I always won. I'm an only
child and I could count on
my mother's vote."

Condoleezza Rice

"Never gonna go a day without you.
Fills me up just thinking
about you. I'll never go a day
without my mama."

Boyz II Men, A Song for Mama

"No one in the world can take the place of your mother. Right or wrong, from her viewpoint you are always right. She may scold you for little things, but never for the big ones."

Harry Truman

"My mother loved children — she would have given anything if I had been one."

Groucho Marx

"My mother is a wonderful, eccentric lady who has no concept whatever of interior monologue. We'll be driving along in the car and she'll suddenly say, 'Ants don't like cucumbers, you know. And roaches don't like cinnamon. Do you want some cheese, Michael?'"

Mike Myers

"I know how to do anything – I'm a mom."

Roseanne Barr

"My mother was the one constant in my life. When I think about my mom raising me alone when she was 20, and working and paying the bills, and, you know, trying to pursue your own dreams, I think it's a feat that is unmatched."

Barack Obama

"Having children just puts the whole world into perspective. Everything else just disappears."

Kate Winslet

"My mother… had a very deep inner spirituality that allowed her to rebuild her life. It's extraordinary that she had such a strong sense of self, and such a commitment to the future, and such a strong creative sense that she could build new worlds for herself and for us out of the total devastation in her life."

Caroline Kennedy

"My mother is my root, my foundation. She planted the seed that I base my life on, and that is the belief that the ability to achieve starts in your mind."

Michael Jordan

"My mother was the most beautiful woman I ever saw. All I am I owe to my mother. I attribute my success in life to the moral, intellectual and physical education I received from her."

George Washington

"There ought to be a hall of fame for mamas, creation's most unique and precious pearl. And heaven help us always to remember that the hand that rocks the cradle rules the world."

Glen Campbell, Hand That Rocks the Cradle

"My mom is the number one person who has taught me to be courteous towards women, to always be respectful and polite to them, and to always lead with your heart."

Zac Efron

"Nobody loves me but my mother.
And she could be jivin' too."

B.B. King

"My mother was a full-time mother.
She didn't have much of her own
career, her own life, her own
experiences. Everything was for her
children. I will never be as good
a mother as she was. She was just
grace incarnate."

Angelina Jolie

"The truth is that no matter how old we are, as long as our mothers are alive, we want our mother."

Goldie Hawn

"The whole motivation for any performer is, 'Look at me, Ma!'"

Lenny Bruce

"My mother taught me to walk proud and tall, as if the world was mine."

Sophie Loren

"My mother's great. She has the major looks. She could stop you from doing anything, through a closed door even, with a single look. Without saying a word, she has that power to rip out your tonsils."

Whoopi Goldberg

"I don't think of myself as a terribly confident person. But I have a survival mechanism that was instilled in me by my mother."

Naomi Watts

"As far as I'm concerned, there's no job more important on the planet than being a mom."

Mark Wahlberg

"Any mother could perform the jobs of several air traffic controllers with ease."

Lisa Alther

"A mother's arms are made of tenderness and children sleep soundly in them."

Victor Hugo

"She made me a security blanket when I was born. That faded green blanket lasted just long enough for me to realize that the security part came from her."

Alexander Crane

"I think, while all mothers deal with feelings of guilt, working mothers are plagued by guilt on steroids!"

Arianna Huffington

"I can remember the first time I had to go to sleep. Mom said, 'Steven, time to go to sleep.' I said, 'But I don't know how.' She said, 'It's real easy. Just go down to the end of tired and hang a left.' So I went down to the end of tired and just out of curiosity I hung a right. My mother was there and she said 'I thought I told you to go to sleep.'"

Steven Wright

"[My mother] always said I was beautiful and I finally believed her at some point."

Lupita Nyong'o

"Back then, I didn't know why, why you were misunderstood. So now I see through your eyes, all that you did was love."

Spice Girls, Mama

"All that I am or ever hope to be, I owe to my angel mother."

Abraham Lincoln

"My mother had a great deal of trouble with me, but I think she enjoyed it."

Mark Twain

"My mother, a high school teacher, never paid that much attention to what anybody else thought about her. So today I feel comfortable making decisions even if other people don't agree."

Soledad O'Brien

"We have a beautiful little girl
who we named after my mom.
In fact, Passive-Aggressive Psycho
turns five tomorrow."

Stewart Francis

"Because I feel that, in the Heavens
above, the angels, whispering to
one another, can find, among their
burning terms of love, none so
devotional as that of 'Mother.'"

Edgar Allen Poe

"A mother's love is patient and forgiving when all others are forsaking, and it never fails or falters, even though the heart is breaking."

Helen Steiner Rice

"My mother is my friend, who shares with me her bread. All my hopelessness cured! Her company makes me secured!"

Israelmore Ayivor

"My mum's so pessimistic that if there was an Olympics for pessimism… she wouldn't fancy her chances."

Nish Kumar

"So when you're lost and you're tired, when you're broken in two, let my love take you higher, 'cause I still turn to you."

Justin Bieber, Turn To You

"The joy that my mom took in having a beautiful house and putting a beautiful meal down in front of us and always having something ready for a guest really inspires me. I used to be sort of messy, but now I laugh at myself, because I kind of like to come home and tidy things up. I'm turning into my mom!"

Jennifer Garner

"I wondered if my smile was as big as hers. Maybe as big. But not as beautiful."

Benjamin Alire Sáenz

"My mother has always been my emotional barometer and my guidance. I was lucky enough to get to have one woman who truly helped me through everything."

Emma Stone

"There shall never be another quite so tender, quite so kind as the patient little mother, nowhere on this earth you'll find her affection duplicated."

Paul C. Brownlow

"I would say that my mother is the single biggest role model in my life, but that term doesn't seem to encompass enough when I use it about her. She was the love of my life."

Mindy Kaling

"A mother! What are worth really? They all grow up whether you look after them or not."

Christina Stead

"Appreciate your mom. She is wiser than you think and stronger than you know. Be thankful."

Steve Maraboli

"A mother's arms are more comforting than anyone else's."

Diana, Princess of Wales

"I can imagine no heroism greater than motherhood."

Lance Conrad

"An ounce of mother is worth a
pound of clergy."

Spanish proverb

"Gilbert put his arm about them.
'Oh, you mothers!' he said. 'You
mothers! God knew what he was
about when he made you."

L.M. Montgomery, Anne's House of Dreams

"God could not be everywhere, so
he created mothers."

Will Leamon

"All those calm, adult discussions, when all she really wanted to do was scream for her momma, her sweet momma, the one person in the world who loved her better than anyone ever would or ever could."

Fannie Flagg

"Great mothers build bridges instead of walls."

Reed Markham

"I like it when my mother smiles.
And I especially like it when
I make her smile."

Adriana Trigiani

"I loved my mother too, I said. I
still do. That's the thing – it never
goes away, even if the person does."

Anna Carey

"Men are what their mothers
made them."

Ralph Waldo Emerson

"I remember my mother's prayers
and they have always followed me.
They have clung to me all my life."

Abraham Lincoln

"My mom is my hero. [She]
inspired me to dream when I was a
kid, so anytime anyone inspires you
to dream, that's gotta be your hero."

Tim McGraw

"I think every working mom probably feels the same thing: you go through big chunks of time where you're just thinking, 'This is impossible – oh, this is impossible.' And then you just keep going and keep going, and you sort of do the impossible."

Tina Fey

"My mom smiled at me. Her smile kind of hugged me."

R.J. Palacio

"My mom is a never-ending song in my heart of comfort, happiness and being. I may sometimes forget the words, but I always remember the tune."

Graycie Harmon

"But behind all your stories is always your mother's story, because hers is where yours begins."

Mitch Albom

"I love being the mother of a two-year-old. It's like being a movie star with no critics."

I Don't Know How She Does It (movie)

"He didn't realize that love as powerful as your mother's for you leaves its own mark."

J.K. Rowling, Harry Potter and the Sorcerer's Stone

"He who loses his mother loses a pure soul who blesses and guards him constantly."

Kahlil Gibran

"I wanna tell the whole world about a friend of mine. This little light of mine, I'm finna let it shine. I'm finna take y'all back to them better times. I'm finna talk about my mama if y'all don't mind."

Kanye West, Hey Mama

"My mom is the greatest mom in the whole wide world. She's done everything for me to make my dreams come true."

Josh Hutcherson

"Life began with waking up and loving my mother's face."

George Eliot

"Most people's mothers are the most influential person in their life. But my mother survived the camps and she was very strong. She made me strong, but she wanted me to be strong. That's more important."

Diane von Furstenberg

"Mother! What a world of affection is comprised in that single word; how little do we in the giddy round of youthful pleasure and folly heed her wise counsels. How lightly do we look upon that zealous care with which she guides our otherwise erring feet, watches with feelings which none but a mother can know the gradual expansion of our youth to the riper years of discretion. We may not think of it then, but it will be recalled to our minds in after years."

Fanny Kelly

Maternal
Words of
Wisdom

"The best academy,
a mother's knee."

James Russell Lowell

"My mom said the only reason
men are alive is for lawn care and
vehicle maintenance."

Tim Allen

"What my mother believed about
cooking is that if you worked hard
and prospered, someone else would
do it for you."

Nora Ephron

"It takes a female to have a baby.
It takes a woman to raise a child.
It takes a mother to raise them
correctly. It takes a warrior to show
them how to change the world."

Shannon L. Alder

"You know Moe, my mom
once said something that really
stuck with me. She said, 'Homer,
you're a big disappointment,' and,
God bless her soul, she was really
onto something."

Homer Simpson

"My momma always said life was like a box of chocolates... you never know what you're gonna get."

Forrest Gump

"Listen carefully to what country people call mother wit. In those homely sayings are couched the collective wisdom of generations."

Maya Angelou

"In the end, mothers are always right. No one else tells the truth."

Randy Susan Meyers

"My mother said the cure for thinking too much about yourself was helping somebody who was worse off than you."

Sylvia Plath

"She taught me what's important and what isn't. And I've never forgotten. And that's what mothers do, I say."

Steven Herrick

"Mama was my greatest teacher, a teacher of compassion, love and fearlessness. If love is sweet as a flower, then my mother is that sweet flower of love."

Stevie Wonder

"Mother always said that honesty was the best policy and money isn't everything. She was wrong about other things too."

Gerald Barzan

"Let France have good mothers,
and she will have good sons."

Napoleon Bonaparte

"My mother once told me, when
you have to make a decision,
imagine the person you want to
become someday. Ask yourself, what
would that person do?"

Barry Deutsch

"My mom gave me the gift of fun and pleasure – she showed me how to enjoy every moment. Another great gift: she was honest about how tough motherhood can be. I can always call her and say, 'It's so hard!' and not feel bad about it."

Felicity Huffman

"Acceptance, tolerance, bravery, compassion. These are the things my mom taught me."

Lady Gaga

"Mama exhorted her children at every opportunity to 'jump at de sun.' We might not land on the sun, but at least we would get off the ground."

Zora Neale Hurston

"My mother taught me to be nice to everybody. And she said something before I left home. She said, 'I want you to always remember that the person you are in this world is a reflection of the job I did as a mother.'"

Jason Segel

"It has been a terrible, horrible, no good, very bad day. My mom says some days are like that."

Judith Viorst

"Took me to school the first day. Taught me how to kneel down and pray. You learned me how to count from one to ten. And never forget, where I've been, momma."

Snoop Dog, I Love My Momma

"My mother used to say that there are no strangers, only friends you haven't met yet. She's now in a maximum security twilight home in Australia."

Dame Edna Everage

"The way we talk to our children becomes their inner voice."

Peggy O'Mara

"A mother enables you to realize that there are different levels of beauty and therein lie the sources of pleasure, some of which are popular and ordinary, and thus of brief value, and others of which are difficult and rare, and hence worth pursuing."

Amy Tan

"As my mom always said, 'You'd rather have smile lines than frown lines.'"

Cindy Crawford

"Giving advice comes naturally to mothers. Advice is in the genes along with blue eyes and red hair."

Lois Wyse

"I always bring my dates to my mother's house for the first date... My mother believes arranged marriages might be able to work... She thinks that if she picked for me that I'd do a lot better."

Jake Gyllenhaal

"I do not understand what makes mothers think they are walking-talking thermometers. But I think somewhere during the process of giving birth and changing diapers, they actually begin to believe they have this supernatural sense."

Melody Carlson

"The mother's heart is a child's schoolroom."

Henry Ward Beecher

"There is no teacher equal
to mother."

Amit Ray

"When you're in the thick of
raising your kids by yourself, you
tend to keep a running list of
everything you think you're doing
wrong. I recommend taking a lot
of family pictures as evidence
to the contrary."

Connie Schultz

Celebrities on
Motherhood

"Motherhood is the most completely humbling experience I've ever had. It puts you in your place, because it really forces you to address the issues that you claim to believe in – and if you can't stand up to those principles when you're raising a child, forget it."

Diane Keaton

"I'm a mother with two small children, so I don't take as much crap as I used to."

Pamela Anderson

"Being a mom made me fear for the first time in my life. The stakes felt huge. I thought I was going to wake up and know exactly what to do, and I was very disappointed when I didn't."

Lisa Kudrow

"I try to call my mother, Betty, with more regularity because I think, what if Hazel didn't call me for two weeks? I'm able to see her mothering now from a different vantage point."

Julia Roberts

"[When] you're dying laughing
because your three-year-old made a
fart joke, it doesn't matter what else
is going on. That's real happiness."

Gwyneth Paltrow

"There's no such thing as
a supermom. We just do the
best we can."

Sarah Michelle Gellar

"The best part of having two babies at once, a son and a daughter, is mostly everything. You're just having that feeling of love inside you all the time and motherhood is such a fulfilling place to be. I kind of wish it would have happened to me earlier in my life."

Jennifer Lopez

"I see myself as mom first. I'm so lucky to have that role in life. The world can like me, hate me or fall apart around me and at least I wake up with my kids and I'm happy."

Angelina Jolie

"My mother hated me. She once took me to an orphanage and told me to mingle."

Phyllis Diller

"I tell my kids, 'I am thinking about you every other minute of my day.'"

Michelle Obama

"There's something that just happens to you when you have a baby, and you look at their little eyes for the first time when you're holding them. They've been safe inside your belly for almost 10 months, and now they're in your arms. Intuition kicks in, where you will do anything for them and you have all the tools inside of you to take care of them."

Hilary Duff

"I have found being a mother has made me emotionally raw in many situations. You heart is beating outside your body when you have a baby."

Kate Beckinsale

"I have to keep reminding myself that I am their mother. Sometimes we are sitting at home and I feel like we are waiting for our mom to come home."

Ruby Wax

"I like my body so much better after I had kids. Is that a crazy thing to say? I'm more womanly. I feel sexier."

Reese Witherspoon

"My mother was a reader and she read to us. She read us *Dr. Jekyll and Mr. Hyde* when I was six and my brother was eight; I never forgot it."

Stephen King

"I may be the only mother in America who knows exactly what their child is up to all the time."

Barbara Bush, mother of former U.S. president George W. Bush

"If I've learned anything as a mom with a daughter who's three, I've learned that you cannot judge the way another person is raising their kid. Everybody is just doing the best they can. It's hard to be a mom."

Maggie Gyllenhaal

"It's been a huge joy, this
experience of being a mom…
I don't know how to articulate it yet,
because it is so fresh."

Claire Danes

"I don't know if I feel like a
bad mom, but at the end of the
day I'm always plagued with did
I do enough? Should I go in a
different direction? But I also know
that my entire life revolves around
[my son] Louis."

Sandra Bullock

"When I had my first child I thought, 'This is the best-kept secret.' You know how parents rattle on to you about, 'Oh, you won't believe your life will never be the same,' and da da da and you think, 'Why can't these people just get over it? All they're doing is yakking on about their kids. It's such a bore.' And then you have kids and you just want to do all the same things."

Uma Thurman

"Sometimes, when I want to take on
the world, I try to remember that
it's just as important to sit down and
ask my son how he's feeling or talk
to him about life."

Angelina Jolie

"I was not a classic mother...
I didn't bake cookies. You can buy
cookies, but you can't buy love."

Raquel Welch

Mothers are Special

"The worst feature of a new baby
is its mother's singing."

Kin Hubbard

"A mother understands what a
child does not say."

Jewish proverb

"If my mom reads that
I'm grammatically incorrect,
I'll have hell to pay."

Larisa Oleynik

"My mother tried to kill me when I was a baby. She denied it. She said she thought the plastic bag would keep me fresh."

Bob Monkhouse

"A mother never realizes that her children are no longer children."

Holbrook Jackson

"I asked mom if I was a gifted child. She said they certainly wouldn't have paid for me."

Bill Watterson, Calvin and Hobbes

"How do I explain her? She's as respected as Mother Theresa, she's as powerful as Stalin, and she's as beautiful as Margaret Thatcher."

Amy Poehler

"I love my mother for all the times she said absolutely nothing."

Erma Bombeck

"I think all mothers are alike, regardless of cultural background, when it comes to illogical cleaning."

Neal Shusterman

"I'm not saying my mother didn't like me, but she kept looking for loopholes in my birth certificate."

Les Dawson

"No one ever died from sleeping in an unmade bed. I have known mothers who remake the bed after their children do it because there is a wrinkle in the spread or the blanket is on crooked. This is sick."

Erma Bombeck

"It is the custom of every good mother after her children are asleep to rummage in their minds and put things straight for next morning, repacking into their proper places the many articles that have wandered during the day. If you could keep awake (but of course you can't) you would see your own mother doing this, and you would find it very interesting to watch her. It is quite like tidying up drawers."

J.M. Barrie

"She never quite leaves her children at home, even when she doesn't take them along."

Margaret Culkin Banning

"Some mothers are kissing mothers and some are scolding mothers, but it is love just the same, and most mothers kiss and scold together."

Pearl S. Buck

"In a child's eyes, a mother is a goddess. She can be glorious or terrible, benevolent or filled with wrath, but she commands love either way. I am convinced that this is the greatest power in the universe."

N. K. Jemisin

"It is not what you do for your children, but what you have taught them to do for themselves, that will make them successful human beings."

Ann Landers

"It's a funny thing about mothers and fathers. Even when their own child is the most disgusting little blister you could ever imagine, they still think that he or she is wonderful."

Roald Dahl

"Whenever my mother talks to me, she begins a conversation as if we were already in the middle of an argument."

Amy Tan

"Living with a teenage daughter is like living with the Taliban: a mum is not allowed to laugh, sing, dance or wear short skirts."

Kathy Lette

"Mom could make small things seem miraculous. That was her talent."

Matthew Quick

"Mothers are multi-taskers."

Sophie Kinsella

"It's the child who's supposed to cry, and the mom who makes it all better, not the other way around, which is why mothers will move heaven and earth to hold it together in front of their own kids."

Jodi Picoult

"Mothers and dogs both had a kind of second sight that made them see into people's minds and know when anything unusual was going on."

Enid Blyton, The Mystery of the Hidden House

"Mothers are basically part of a scientific experiment to prove that sleep is not a crucial part of human life."

Anon

"Mothers can forgive anything! Tell me all, and be sure that I will never let you go, though the whole world should turn from you."

Louisa May Alcott